CRAZY WITH A SIDE OF HAPPY

STORIES OF A HOUSEWIFE'S FUNNY FAILS

KRISTA GARRAND

BOOK SUMMARY

ABANDONING her full-time job to dedicate time to her children, Krista includes you on her journey of learning how to navigate the excitement of stay-at-home motherhood. She quickly learns that while she is artsy, organized and great at conversation, she isn't particularly domesticated. Writing and photography skills do nothing to help with cooking and child rearing. Laugh with her as she jokes about feeling less and less like a successful, smart woman and more like Amelia Bedelia.

For my babies... for making me a little bit more crazy, a little less cool and a lot more happy.

CHAPTER 1

WELCOME TO MOTHERHOOD

SO, today I learned that it's true. It being, one of my biggest fears since learning that I was *really* pregnant. It's true that hospitals really do give people babies without instructions. *Real babies!* Not those fake babies that you wind up and make poop by feeding it colored pellets, or the ones you get in sex-education class that cry constantly, bringing you to the brink of insanity. No, the hospital gives you real-live babies, with organs, nerves and feelings. A real human being. One that you're responsible for without the first piece of instruction on what to do.

Apparently, as a mother, you're just supposed to know these things. Females are supposed to be born with instinctive knowledge about their young. You know, maternal instincts? Riiiight.

I really thought I might have those so-called maternal instincts, but since I was given a premature baby to bring home, I'm completely clueless and winging it.

That's right, my baby is premature. He just spent a ridiculous amount of time in the Neonatal Intensive Care Unit, or what us cool people like to call the NICU. Now that he is growing and sustaining, they sent him home with me, the idiot, non-instinctive mother who doesn't know what to do.

"Don't stimulate him," they told me. "He'll burn calories." So, today, in the spirit of not stimulating him, I've sat next to where he slept and watched him breathe. I silently prayed the entire time for him to continue sleeping.

Please don't wake up, little baby. Please just sleep. Mommy has no idea what to do with you if you open those sweet blue eyes.

Of course since I'm mostly unlucky and because as I stated earlier, he's a real, live human being, he did wake up before I was ready for him to. I think I handled the first few times okay, but the fourth time he woke up was what I think I'll forever consider my initiation into motherhood. It was that single moment where I knew that my life had jack-knifed and turned into a different direction. That moment when I could finally say, with one of those cool-kid hashtags and everything: #YouKnowYou'reAMomWhen.

It started out as a normal routine of checking off all the things I'm supposed to check. Starting with his diaper. Is it wet? Yes. So, I commenced the four-thousandth diaper change.

I laid him down on a changing pad on my bed, because you know, since he was preemie, we didn't have a changing table yet. I had his clean diaper and a pack of wipes next to him, ready to rock and roll. It started out simple enough. Open the diaper, lift his teeny-tiny tush to pull away the dirty diaper, grab a wipe, clean him up, grab the clean diaper, lift his teeny-tiny tush again and –

Oh no, he just pooped. Oh my god, it just shot out and... what is that on my... is it...?

Is it on my face?!

OH MY GOD HE POOPED ON MY FACE!

That's right... I lifted his little bum and apparently aimed his little sphincter right at the side of my face, giving him the perfect opportunity to projectile-poop across the foot of distance separating us and onto my face.

I jerked my hand away from his tiny little legs, succeeding in knocking the package of wipes onto the floor and completely out of my reach. So, like the sad loser that I am, I stood there helpless, not knowing what to do. Poop was stuck to my cheek right below my eye and smeared across the length of my face, ending at the bottom of my ear lobe. Stupid gravity assisted with it sliding down my skin and dripping off my ear and onto my shoulder.

Seriously, what are you supposed to do in a moment like this when there is literally shit on your freaking face? For a few seconds, I provided my few week old son with a view of his first dance as I toyed with the idea of sprinting to the bathroom to wipe it off my face.

I stepped backward, towards the direction of the bath-room, but froze when I realized that I'd have to let go of his legs. *What if he falls? What if he rolls over for the first time while I run for some tissue?*

I stepped back towards him, then as I continued to hold onto his ankles, I reached with my foot to the package of wipes. Of course, I wasn't close to reaching them at all. Not in the slightest.

Looking down at him, feeling the poo-goop continuing to slide down my face, I gritted my teeth and considered using the collar of my shirt to wipe off the poop. But geez, then it would be on my neck and chest, so really I wouldn't be removing the poop at all. Instead, I'd be spreading it across my upper body and likely be creating a situation that I'd have to endure for longer than necessary.

What if I wipe it on my shirt, then he screams for the next hour and I can't take time to wash it off? Then I'll be walking around with poop on my face, shirt and neck.

I glanced behind me again, looking at the bathroom in longing, realizing that I was going to have to just suck it up and change his diaper while shit was coating a large portion of my face.

With a huff, I decided that leaving your baby unattended on the bed was a mommy no-no, so I chose to continue diapering him, forcing myself to just allow my son's mustard colored poop to slowly drip off my face like melting ice cream.

Freaking gross!

Once he was clean, I placed him in his bassinet quicker than ever before and sprinted towards the bathroom, feeling movement of my body cause the poop to drop in big glops onto my shoulder. By the time I reached the sink, I had a sheen of yellow poo-goop on the side of my face, my ear lobe, and a mountain on my shoulder.

I jerked my shirt off, like the true idiot that I am, succeeding in smearing the poop mountain into my hair. An entire sentence of expletives ricocheted off my skull as I threw my shirt onto the floor.

I turned on the shower, feeling eager and impatient to rid my skin of my son's stool, just as he started to scream.

Briefly, I considered kicking the tub, but luckily I reconsidered, realizing that I'd probably only end up breaking my toe. I turned off the shower, then stomped over to the sink and stuck my head under the faucet.

The warm water began to wash away the poop from the side of my hair and I would have been happy about that, if the poop wasn't draining down the side of my face.

Oh my goodness! No! It's draining down the side of my face! No, no, no, no!

I closed my eyes tight and pressed my lips firmly together as the poop water coated my face. Deciding that this couldn't possibly get any worse, and because my son's screaming was becoming shrill, I used my hand to rub the poop off my ear, cheek and chin too.

Once the water began to run clear, instead of yellow, I pulled away, then used a wash rag to remove it from my neck and chest.

For the rest of the day, even when I resumed my spot watching him sleep, all I could think about was the poop particles that were still in my hair and coating my skin. I imagined that Clorox commercial, where they show the bacteria and germs magnified, knowing that teeny, tiny, microscopic poop bacteria was currently thriving in the strands of my hair and on the surface of my skin.

Yeah... Welcome to Motherhood, Krista. It's freaking awesome.

CHAPTER 2

YOU'LL TURN INTO A FISH

I REFUSE to believe that I'm the only parent that's lied to her kid before. We've all done it. We've told our kids that the store doesn't sell replacement batteries for that super loud, incredibly annoying toy they love. We've told them that if the ice cream truck is playing music, it means they've run out of ice cream. Or, my personal favorite, that when you lie your ears turn red.

We've all done it and most of us admit it proudly. Usually, I admit it proudly too, because hey, who am I kidding, the lies work! Well, except for this one time. This one time that I told one of these lies that backfired, then blew up in my face.

You see, my toddler had a love obsession with splashing the water in the bath time. Obviously, I didn't share that love and despised the obsession. Simply telling a two-year-old no doesn't always work, so naturally, I tried to use a little white lie in an effort to stop the intense splashing.

Perhaps I could have dealt with this issue a little better, if his splashing didn't include dumping large cups of water on his head, then proceeding to choke on the water as it poured into his open, giggling little mouth. But, every time he choked on water, then screamed as though the water was shredding his esophagus, I cringed and loathed it more and more.

So, one night, as he was splashing away, oblivious to the river he was making outside of the tub, I told him, "AJ, if you keep splashing like that and dumping water onto your head, you're going to turn into a fish."

He froze.

He dropped the cup.

And I thought to myself, *Yes! It worked! I'm so awesome at this mom stuff! I should have another kid!*

Then, suddenly, during that moment while I was bestowing gleeful, silent praise upon myself, he opened his mouth, letting out a sound that reminded me of all the lost souls screaming in the deepest pits of hell.

He screamed so loudly, my ear drums literally rang, then proceeded to panic and attempt to crawl out of the tub.

"No fish! No fish!" he screamed, as he kicked and thrashed around. Of course, water was sloshing out of the tub like waves at the beach, creating an even bigger mess than before.

Shoot! I freaking suck at this! Why did I say that!

I tried comforting him, feeling like an idiot, realizing that I couldn't really take back what I said because then he'd see me for the liar that I was. I couldn't have that. I needed him to believe my next lie when it was time for me to tell it.

I fretted, wondering what I should say next.

Should I tell him that he will only turn into a fish if he does it again? Or, will that just remind him that turning into a fish is a possibility, then scare him more?

Oh my God, my kid is never going to take a bath again!

"It's okay," I soothed him, all while I was rinsing off the

soap with frantic hands, wanting to get him out of the tub as soon as I could.

"No fish! No Fish!" he screamed at me.

Shaking my head, I rinsed him again. He shrieked like I had tossed boiling water on his back. "Nooo Mommy! No make me a fish!"

"You won't turn into a fish this time, baby. Just don't splash the water and pour it on your head again, okay?"

My husband came running upstairs, thinking that something was horribly wrong. And, well duh, he was right. He married an idiot who gives his kid a complex about taking a damn bath.

I assured him that everything was fine, while deep down wondering if AJ would ever take a bath again without being terrified.

Is there a name for being afraid of the bath? I bet there is. If there is a phobia for being afraid of the moon, then there has got to be a phobia for being afraid of taking a bath. And, because of my lack of brilliance and eagerness to lie, my son will have me to thank for giving him said phobia.

I'll have to google this to find out the name of this phobia so that when he's old enough and he smells like a walking, talking armpit, I can educate him about the pain I have inflicted upon him and explain why his stench is so strong.

Inwardly, I'm shaking my head at myself, rolling my eyes and swatting my own hand with a ruler. I super suck.

AJ's fear of becoming a fish lasted for a few days. Okay, I'm not being honest, it really lasted for almost a week. Finally, after battling him, I finally decided to tell him that Mommy was wrong and that he wasn't going to turn into a fish.

It didn't matter that I had decided to be honest. He still

thought he'd turn into a fish and screeched anytime we touched his head with water.

My mother, to this day almost five years later, still laughs at me about this. She finds humor in the fact that I succeeded in scaring the wits out of my child in my failed attempt to just be a normal, lying-through-my-damn-teeth-to-get-you-to-listen parent.

CHAPTER 3

AN EAGLE IN THE SKY

I THINK in one of my novels, I wrote from the perspective of one of my beloved characters that the universe was a bitch. I wrote them during an impassioned part of the story, hoping that the readers could find humor in the sarcastic truth about unlucky folks like myself who would be without luck entirely if it weren't for the bad, sadistic kind of luck. I literally stole those words from my own thoughts. Those four words found their way together the day I birthed my second child.

My startlingly unexpected second child, despite his colorful and mostly challenging personality, is the light of my life. The bitchy universe gave him to me, in what feels like mockery or jest most days. This little sour-patch boy stubbornly forced his way into my life, and planted himself right into my heart, where he belongs.

I'll really have to thank the universe some day...

But before he planted himself there, before the day he was born and I decided that the universe was a mean bitch that liked to laugh at and mock me, I had a completely different idea about what my lively little Zachary would be.

You see, my first child, who at the time was about two years old, was what every mother dreams about when she thinks about having kids. Although he made quite the dramatic entrance with his surprisingly early arrival, he lacked drama in every other way that mattered. He was and still is very serene and thrives on structure. The kid seriously teeters close to perfect most days. He's a dream and as soon as he turned two, I was ready to create a female version of that dream.

During Zachary's pregnancy, I convinced myself that I was carrying exactly what I craved and wanted. My new baby was going to be a sweet, calm, quiet little girl with strawberry blond hair and blue eyes.

Nothing prepared me for what I actually birthed and within a four second time span, I had to get over my dream of having the perfect little girl and accept that the universe was enjoying the little joke it had bestowed upon me.

The sweet calm little girl I wanted came out as an angry, very loud, chubby cheeked little boy with the lungs of a toddler. He looked exactly like me and seemed to be maintaining my temper too, because he had no qualms about expressing his irritation at being bothered. He was absolutely nothing like the sweet, quiet little person that his brother was. He was a literal opposite.

That startling realization hit me for the first time when he really cried. Not the throat clogged, frantic cry that is expected when he was born, but the first real cry that was laced with what sounded a lot like anger.

There I was, laying in my hospital bed, feeling a bit guilty for being grateful that everyone had finally left and gave me some time to sleep. Zachary, only a few hours old, was laying in his clear plastic bassinet sleeping and my mom was sitting in the chair next to me. The room was silent, finally.

I closed my eyes, reveling in the feeling of being relaxed for the first time in hours. It's tough to relax with a gaping hole in your lower abdomen held together by glue, staples and stitches, but with a silent room, I was eager to try, when all of a sudden it happened.

The shrill sound of my son's cry echoed through the room, bouncing violently off the walls and ricocheting off my ear drums. It jolted me and in my surprised state, I almost ripped a staple right out of my skin, and I think, it may have possibly catapulted me into fight-or-flight mode for a few agonizing seconds.

Most mothers think their baby's first cries are the most adorable and melodic sounds on earth. I was one of those mothers once upon a time, when my oldest son's cry sounded like a tiny baby lamb. The sound was adorable and such a wonderful sound that I was eager to hear it again.

Zachary's cry, however, wasn't pleasant in any type of way. It wasn't adorable and it certainly wasn't anything I ever wanted to hear again.

It was as though the universe was literally laughing, in that deep, belly laugh kind of way that vibrates your chest a little bit.

As I said, the shrill screeching sound jolted me, so my eyes burst open and I looked over at my mom with my mouth gaping open.

"Oh my god! Go get him! Pick him up!" I yelled at her.

"Oh my god!" she shouted back, frantically rising to her feet and picking him up.

"What's wrong with him?" I cried, wincing as his screeching got louder and louder. It was the most awful, ear piercing sound that seemed to rattle the walls.

"I don't know!" she yelled back at me, her eyes wide and her brows raised exceptionally high.

I felt like we were racing, like we had merely seconds available to figure out what was wrong with this little baby before his shrieks caused him to combust.

"Is he wet?! Did he poop?! *Mom!* Check if he pooped!"

She looked over at me, with this incredulous expression as if to say, *What the hell do you think I'm doing?!*

"I am!" she yelled back at me.

The screeching continued, sounding exactly like an eagle in the sky. What exactly is the sound that an eagle makes called anyway? I don't know. What I do know, is that it's a loud, painful sound, one that you can feel in the marrow of your bones and that my son sounded *exactly* like it as he continued to scream.

After discovering that he did in fact poop, my mom provided him the quickest diaper change of his life, then, like she was playing a game of hot potato, she thrust him over to me like she was afraid of the little booger.

We looked at each other for a second or two, absorbing the quiet and reflecting on what had just happened, then both burst into laughter.

"What the hell kind of cry was that?" she asked through her laughter. "Oh my god that was loud!"

I laughed, letting tears spill from my eyes, because what else could I do? His evil sounding cry should have been expected after all I went through during his pregnancy. I should have known he was going to be a crazy, demanding little boy from day one. He gave me every single pregnancy symptom in the damn book, every single day of his gestation. I really should have expected that when he made his grand entrance, he'd behave the same way. A little crazy and a lot demanding.

It was funny at first. You know, laughing at all the examples of how different Zachary and AJ were and how much of a handful he was going to be. I spent countless times chuckling and laughing at how hilarious it was that I got exactly the opposite of what I wanted. A boy, with brown hair, who was temperamental and seemed to have a short fuse.

My mother joked that I should enjoy his infancy while it lasted, because he was going to be a beast when he got older.

Man oh man, she was right. Today, at three years old he *is* a beast. A crazy, funny, hot-heated little beast in a china shop, running our house with his demanding little attitude and silly laughter. He is the epitome of a boy. All rough and tumble, forever dirty and getting into things, excitable and loud.

Who knew I could love an insane, crazy little person so much? I really wonder sometimes, was my life dull before Zachary? Like, what did I do? Who did I chase and run after? Whose billion questions did I answer? Who was there to make me laugh? And, were there no disasters, ever?

It's funny, even though it's really kind of not. Regardless of his level of craziness, I love that little stinker so much it hurts. He's just as sweet as he is sour.

My very own little sour-patch kid.

I joke sometimes that if he would have been my first child, he would likely have been my only. The child wears me out so completely every day that I'm worthless when the moon rises.

And, even at three years old, when he decides to be his demanding little self, I still react just as though he is shrieking like an eagle in the sky on some days, feeling frantic and increasing in pace.

Really, it's impossible not to. He has conditioned me to react that way and honestly, I'm not sure if I could refrain if I tried.

CHAPTER 4

DISPOSING OF ANTS

AFTER EACH MEAL, I have developed a very necessary routine of sweeping the floor. I'm sure all mothers of toddlers partake in this particular chore, especially if they have a monstrous, rule-breaking toddler like mine. Zachary still has a horrible habit of throwing half of his food onto the floor, despite my reminders, sweet talking attempts, idle threats and even bribery, so sweeping multiple times a day is a must.

After breakfast one morning, I began to sweep the floor. I instructed AJ to pick up his toys - and yes, there are toys underneath the table. I am not Martha Stewart, my house is not spotless, I am a real mom with real kids that make a mess. There are toys everywhere. Don't judge me.

Anyway, I asked AJ to pick up his toys so they wouldn't get swept into the trash. He immediately started screaming, and it wasn't the kind of scream that was because his toys were seconds from landing next to poopy diapers in the trash can... no, it was the kind of scream that jolts a hover mom like me into high-gear.

My helicopter and I were there in a flash to see what

bone had been broken. Okay, no broken bones... but there was still a reason to panic because *Holy freaking crap*, there were ANTS EVERYWHERE. The floor, the baseboards, the wall... even, AJ's feet were covered in ants. I picked him up and ran over to the sink to rinse them off. I must have entered fight or flight mode because I was very speedy, and probably a little frantic. After cleaning AJ's feet off, I placed him on the couch and instructed him not to move.

Now what do I do? There are ants everywhere....

It looked like someone had stomped into an ant pile the way they were scattered all over my floor. They were crawling on my curtain, the carpet, the baseboards, the walls and up my sliding glass doors... all after a half chewed skittle and a petrified french fry underneath my table.

WHAT SHOULD I DO?! OH I KNOW! - THE VACUUM CLEANER! ***BRILLIANT!!***

In a flash, I had run upstairs, retrieved my husband's super fancy, very expensive vacuum cleaner and set to work. Feeling pretty proud of myself for such a clever disposal of ants, I vacuumed those suckers up in a jiffy.

AJ cheered me on, while Zachary watched me with curious little toddler eyes from his highchair seat. I thought to myself, *I'm getting pretty good at this housewife, mom stuff,* as I ran the vacuum's hose across every ant inside of my house.

After each ant was successfully sucked into my canister vacuum, I decided to be really thorough and go outside to suck up the rest off the porch. If you're going to do a job, might as well be thorough and do it right!

After I finished, I carried my vacuum cleaner back inside. I was barely in the door and Zachary was crying. I wasn't surprised since I had been out of his eyesight for more than thirty seconds, something he simply cannot tolerate. I set the vacuum down near the sliding glass door, left the hose on the floor and went to him.

My nose immediately crinkled. There was definitely a poop smell. I sighed, refraining from laughter at how perfect my son's timing was. It's par for the course in this house to have everything happen at the absolute worst possible time.

Now that my body had successfully abandoned my frantic, fight-or-flight state of mind, I took my time lifting Zachary out of his chair and changing his diaper. I even took time to blow raspberries on his chubby little belly, you know, since I had no way of knowing that my house was still under attack by ants.

As I entered the kitchen on my way to dispose of the diaper, I noticed ants again.

REALLY?! How did they come back so fast?

As I knelt down to inspect, a light bulb switched on in my head... and immediately with severe dread, I realized my mistake.

Ants are living things...

I have a canister vacuum...

Of course they're going to CRAWL OUT.

In the short few minutes it took me to change a diaper, ants had invaded my eat-in-kitchen again. They were crawling out of the vacuum everywhere... out of the hose, out of the front where the beater bar is, out of the canister itself, as if to say, "Nice try moron! We're back!"

OH MY GOODNESS! WHAT DO I DO NOW?! I KNOW, CALL LARISA SHE WILL KNOW.

Larisa, my best friend and seasoned housecleaner, offered me lots of laughter and only one method to rid my vacuum of all the ants.

Really, all I can do is leave it outside and let them crawl out? There must be another way... I'll call my mom, she'll know what to do. Shoot, no answer. Okay, I'll call my Aunt. Great - more laughter... same response. Okay, fine, I'll leave the damn vacuum outside for a bit.

I turned the vacuum back on, sucked them back into the canister and bolted outside as quickly as I could. If someone was watching me, they surely would have thought I was in a relay race or something... I was speedy and focused. I had the vacuum cleaner outside and the canister off and flying through the air in about ten seconds flat!

Great, now I not only just scattered ants all over my yard but my husband's fancy vacuum canister and filter are probably broken now as they're lying in the dirt. Oh well, I'll leave it there for a while and let the ants crawl out, then go check on it.

The next morning, we woke up to the beginning of an ice storm. Lots of rain and ice and rain and more ice.

My first thought was, *oops- the vacuum cleaner is outside.*

My husband wasn't too pleased that we have to get a new one, but hey it never hurts to get an upgrade... right?

Right.

CHAPTER 5

A VALENTINE'S DAY CAKE

SO, for Valentine's Day I decided to bake for my husband. My husband had a mother that baked things for him from scratch all his life and while he's never stated it, I think he misses having baked goods in the kitchen. I thought my idea was epic and thoughtful, despite the fact that I have never baked before. Well, not alone at least. My first baking experience was supervised and I really didn't do anything that could actually be considered baking, AJ and my mom did basically everything, so it honestly doesn't count. I knew that I was certainly not ready to do anything from scratch, so I bought the kind in the box. I thought to myself, this should be easy, right?

I went to the grocery store in search of vanilla cake and vanilla icing. No, vanilla isn't my husband's favorite, but if I'm baking a cake I want some and since I can't have caffeine, vanilla seems to be the way to go.

Let me just get to the point and say that the baking aisle is overwhelming. Seriously. I just wanted regular vanilla cake mix, but they have yellow, butter golden, white, white marble, lemon, moist yellow and so many more. I thought to myself... *oh my goodness, which one is regular vanilla? Is vanilla not a cake flavor? Okay, I guess I'll get the butter golden? Or white? Is white actually vanilla flavored or does that taste like buttercream? Wait, is buttercream vanilla or would that be the butter golden? If buttercream is actually butter golden, why don't they just call it buttercream? Yeah, buttercream must be butter golden, I guess that makes sense... no, that can't be because there is buttercream over there... okay, I'll just get the butter golden, it must be good since that lady over there just got some too. I mean, why can't they just have one freaking flavor? Does it have to be so complicated?*

Okay, so now I needed icing, just regular vanilla icing. My mind was immediately overwhelmed again because they don't have just regular vanilla, they have creamy vanilla, whipped vanilla, fluffy white, buttercream, snow-white buttercream, vanilla with sprinkles, cream cheese, light vanilla... it goes on and on! I just wanted regular vanilla icing!

Why are there so many? What is the difference between whipped and creamy? Does snow-white buttercream taste different than regular buttercream or is it just a color difference? Maybe I should just get buttercream since I got buttercream cake. Wait, I didn't get buttercream cake, I got butter golden. Maybe I should just get buttercream cake? Oh man, I need to hurry up because this lady is near me and waiting, I better look like I know what I'm doing... I'll just grab something real quick and go with it - Okay, there is chocolate. Chocolate it is!

I exited the baking aisle with sweat on my brow and headed towards the bakery. *He loves snickerdoodle cookies, so I'll just buy those. I'm not standing in that baking aisle for another half hour!*

Well, to my dismay they actually didn't have snickerdoodle cookies made, so I headed back in the direction of the wretched baking aisle. Maybe he doesn't need cookies too? I was excited to find some snickerdoodle mix in a little pre-mixed baggy. This should be easy, only three of my own ingredients needed. Sold! Glad that wasn't as difficult as the cake.

Once I got home, I decided to make the cookies first since it was quicker. I read the instructions twice and got to work. And let me ask all the other moms who bake: Why does it have to be so hard to mix this stuff? I was using back muscles trying to evenly mix the ingredients! Sheesh!

Everything was going smoothly until it gave me an option for my cookie size. I could do regular or large. *What? How big is regular? Or large? Is there a size chart on this thing?* Of course, there was nothing to help me figure out how big or small a regular size cookie should be. *Okay, I guess I'll just wing it. How big were the dough balls that my mom made before? This big? Nah, I think they were bigger... hmmm... that looks about right.*

Apparently my selected cookie size was not in fact regular. It must have been large, or maybe even extra large because all of my cookies stuck together. It looked like rolls coming out of the oven.

Crap! I should have spread them farther apart! What do I do now? Maybe if I just separate them before they cool it will be okay.

So, I quickly took the hot cookies out of the pan so they would be separate instead of all together. I learned this was wrong. My cookies tore apart, were misshapen and looked a little mutilated when I got them on my pretty cookie tray.

Dammit. What did I do wrong? I followed all of the directions.

I sent Whitney a picture, my other best friend who is a seasoned baker. I was still pretty proud that I didn't burn them. Her response was, "Did you let them cool?"

Did I let them cool?

No! I didn't know to let them cool! Nobody told me to do that. How was I supposed to know? It didn't say that on the baggy! What happened to warm cookies fresh out of the oven? How are those possible if you have to let the damn things cool before you touch them?

I was thoroughly confused. I even went and pulled the cookie bag out of the trash to re-read the instructions and there is was, at the very bottom, "Cool completely before removing from cookie sheet."

DAMMIT!

I brought my mutilated looking cookies to my husband anyway. He of course laughed at me as he ate them and told me they were perfect. What a sweet little liar he is.

He must love me.

I waited until he went to work to attempt the cake. It looked much more complicated and required more ingredients. Everything was actually going pretty smooth, even when I mixed everything, although I did decide that I was going to ask for an electric whisk because doing it by hand really started to hurt my poor, delicate little muscles.

I was feeling pretty proud of myself as I poured my batter into the pan. As I read the box to figure out how long it should cook, I was confused again. The bake time apparently is contingent on your pan size. How am I supposed to know what pan size this is? Ugh! It's not like I have a ruler or a measuring tape handy.

I'll call my mom.

After explaining the options the box gives, "Eight-inch, nine-inch, thirteen by nine-inch, bunt or twenty-four cupcakes," I asked her what size my pan was. She of course laughed because how the hell should she know over the phone? Is it round or square she asks? Then she tells me that it's usually engraved on the pan. *WELL NOT ON MINE! Well, maybe it is and I just can't see it since I already poured my batter in... dammit.*

I tell her I have one round pan the size of a volleyball and one the size of a basketball. She continues to laugh at me and tells me to use the one that's the size of the volleyball. I ask her, "Do you think that's an eight or nine inch?" She believes it's probably eight, but can't be sure. I decided to just go with the bake time for the eight inch... it was the shortest bake time. I could always bake a little longer if that's wrong, right?

So, I set my timer for twenty-two minutes. She also asked me if I had toothpicks. No? What the heck do I need toothpicks for while baking a cake?

Twenty-two minutes later, I opened my oven and excitedly began to remove my cake. I figured it probably wasn't good if it was sloshing around, so I put it back in. Ten minutes later, I tried again... it looked, ready-ish.

Ugh, who am I kidding I have no idea what a cake is supposed to look like without icing!

I looked at the box for guidance and read, "Cake is done when a toothpick inserted in the center comes out clean." Ohhhhhh! *That's* what I need a toothpick for!

Okay, well do I have toothpicks? Crap!

Luckily I did have toothpicks. I pushed on it and smooshed the top of my cake.

Oops... guess I wasn't supposed to push that hard. I

thought the toothpick had to go all the way to the bottom. Oh well, I'll just cover it with icing.

This time, I let my baked treat cool. The box told me to. I read it twice.

Once it was cool, I turned the pan upside down to get the cake out. Nothing happened. I shook it a little. Still nothing. *Why isn't it coming out?* Ugh! I shook it harder. Still nothing. I put the pan back down and tried to pry it out with a spoon. I succeeded, but my cake matched my cookies... it was mutilated.

It's okay, I'll fix it with icing.

I wasn't giving up yet. I thought for sure I could just piece my cake back together with my chocolate icing.

WRONG.

Let me just tell you, in case you don't already know. Cake icing is not like putty, it doesn't hold things together. Actually, the more you try to spread the icing to hold the cake together, the more the cake breaks apart. Yep. That is a fact.

Lesson learned.

So, I finished icing my misshapen, crumbling cake. It looked like a first grader did it. Icing everywhere, sloppy, uneven...

I'll just tell my husband that I let AJ ice it. That's believable, right? Three year olds ice cakes...

I was almost done. I just needed to write on it. I decided when I was at the store that I didn't need to buy that fancy frosting that you write with, I had some left over from Christmas when we made cookies. I felt proud of myself for being resourceful and saving money while I made my decision at the store and quickly felt silly and defeated when I learned, again, that I was wrong.

Cookie icing and cake icing are very different, in case

you didn't know that either. And when you're trying to write "Happy Valentines Day," on a small, probably eight inch round cake, you should probably start with small letters.

I didn't and now my cake says 'Happy Valentin' in VERY sloppy letters.

It's the thought that counts right?

CHAPTER 6

SLEEP BABY, SLEEP!

OKAY, before I even start this chapter I just want to warn those with weak stomachs that this chapter is not for you. Seriously, if you're offended by odors, comments that may not be one hundred percent politically correct, bodily fluids, or anything that could be considered gross please do not read it. Skip ahead to the next chapter, right now. I'm not going to apologize for it, I won't feel sorry that you were offended or grossed out...

You have been warned.

So, I feel it important to vent if you will... to laugh at a particularly frustrating part about being a parent, because honestly, there isn't anything else I can do at this point. Sometimes, I swear I could be the star of a really cheesy sitcom, because my life has all the makings of slapstick humor. I can just imagine people piling in front of their televisions at eight o'clock to laugh at the dumbest, smart person they've ever seen.

A few days prior to this frustrating parent experience, the boys and I had been sick. We swap germs like cool baseball cards and keep runny noses in style, so it isn't shocking on any level that we weren't well.

Any parent knows how challenging it is to be there for your kids, to be happy and silly and "on" when you feel like crap. It's even worse when your children also feel like crap and are needy, whiny and clingy.

Let's just say that weeks like this one certainly don't fall anywhere close to my favorites list. As if that wasn't fantabulous enough, Zachary had started to challenge me during bed time and during his sickness, his challenge had gotten considerably worse.

There was a time that I could lay him in his room and he would go right to sleep, but now he requires me to rock him, sing to him, soothe him... and do anything *he* is in the mood for on that particular night to go to sleep. Sometimes, that takes hours.

Yes, HOURS.

As parents, I'm sure we have all experienced that moment when your baby is finally drifting off to sleep. That moment where you're forced to try to breathe silently, you're still as a statue, you don't DARE make a move. You just sit there doing consistently whatever it was that you were doing to make him fall asleep... you change NOTHING.

Well, that is the moment that my little tale will start:

After fighting Zachary for about an hour and a half, he finally started drifting off to sleep. I was feeling more grateful than I normally would have, because I was so dreadfully tired. He had refused to nap, he was whiny and didn't want to be put down that entire day, which of course didn't even give me a second of a break. I also felt particularly challenged because my nose was stuffed up but running at the same time. Don't you hate that?

Anyway, he finally started to breathe a little heavy. We were in his glider rocker swaying back and forth, he was laying with his tummy pressed against me, his head cradled in the crook of my elbow and I had been patting his butt with my left hand for a *very* long time. So long, that I could feel the muscles in my wrist aching a little. At that moment, my nose started running...

And because of my perpetual bad luck, there was nothing I could do, both of my hands were positioned on him, I was *not* going to move to wipe it and risk waking him up. Of course I couldn't make any noise, so trying to inhale did me no good. I was forced to just let it be.

I stopped patting his butt for a second just to see if he noticed. Of course he did, he twitched. So, snot water be damned, I continued to pat his chubby butt and pretend I wasn't leaking liquid mucus down my face.

Is this seriously happening right now?! Is there really SNOT WATER dripping on my lip?! Great, now it's tickling so much that it feels like it's itching!

I tried to wiggle my nose to alleviate the itch, it didn't work, it just made the snot water drop onto my bottom lip.

Still rocking him ever so gently and at the same speed while still patting his butt, I just let it happen. That's right, I let the freaking snot water drop onto my mouth. It's this type of moment in my sitcom that would queue the canned laughter and likely a recorded, fake applause. I mean, seriously, has this ever happened to anyone else or is it just me? Have I just been blessed with the worst luck ever or do I somehow unintentionally bring this on myself?

I tried to squeeze my lips together tightly so that none of the snot water could get into my mouth.

Great, now it's on both of my lips and now dropping onto

my chin... I cannot believe this is happening to me. What do I do?

As it started to drip off of my chin and onto my chest, I decided that I couldn't take it anymore. I was going to take the risk of placing him in his bed. Honestly, it would cause less movement than trying to free my hands and wipe my face, so putting him in his bed seemed like the best option.

So, I slowed the speed of the rocker and very slowly started to stand.

YES! I'm standing and he is still asleep! Okay, just a few feet to the bed.

I was so focused on his bed that I didn't notice his stuffed puppy below my feet. And, of course it couldn't have been an ordinary stuffed puppy, it had to be a stuffed *talking* puppy, you know, the one that sings, counts and teaches A,B,C's... it was THAT puppy. As I started to bend over to lay him in bed, I kicked that stupid puppy right in the face and in retaliation it shouted, "YOU'RE MY FRIEND DO-DO-DO-DO-DO!"

Are you freaking kidding me?! REALLY?! Of course Zachary's eyes opened immediately and he started to whine. UGH.

A slew of very bad curse words catapulted through my mind as I walked back to the damn rocking chair with snot water still dripping down my face.

I spent another half hour in the rocking chair getting him to sleep and no, I didn't have a chance to wipe my face. So yes, I still had snot water running down my mouth. Actually, I had a little puddle of snot water on my chest where it dripped that whole time. I finally decided to try again, this time I made sure I knew exactly where that puppy was. As I bent down to lay him on his bed, my snot water started to drop faster...

OMG, why is this happening to me right now?! It's dripping at a high rate of speed while I'm forced to slowwwwwly lay him down.

YES! Success! I did it!

I bolted out of his room straight towards the bathroom to retrieve a baby wipe to clean myself off, whacking my toe on the door frame in the process.

Dammmmmmit!! *REALLY?! What's next? Is the damn house going to catch fire?!*

So, naturally, in true Krista form, once my face was clean, I sat down to write this chapter for you all to laugh at with an aching toe and a tissue stuffed in my nose to stop the dripping.

But hey, I'll take it... it was gross, but at least my baby was finally asleep— perhaps with my snot water droplets either on his footie pajamas or on his bed– but he was asleep nevertheless. And at that moment, THAT is what was important.

As I sat and reflected on what had happened, I felt it necessary to point out that I knew becoming a parent meant I'd need to sacrifice some things for the sake of my children's happiness, well-being or health.... but, this particular sacrifice is just flat out unreasonable. Seriously.

CHAPTER 7

20 QUESTIONS? TRY 1,000

THOSE WHO KNOW me are very familiar with one fact about me: I am not a patient person. Becoming a stay-at-home-mom has forced me to pull patience out of the deepest depths of my soul so that I don't lose my mind and end up on the news.

Those parents who have children between the ages of three and five can relate to the typical inquisitive child. I unfortunately couldn't just have a *typical* inquisitive child, no... I had to birth a child that would tease the boundaries of my patience and control, owning the stereotypical labels of 'curious' and 'inquisitive' to the letter. As if having a dreadfully curious child wasn't enough to keep me fully busy and randomly entertained by my failed methods to maintain control, I decided to push myself even farther so that I am now hanging off the proverbial ledge of control by my fingernails. Being the never-satisfied-so-I-need-more kind of woman that I am, I decided to birth a second child, a mocking bird if you will, who has a life's mission to mimic everything his older, curiously verbose brother does... also to the letter.

So, in true Krista-fashion, I decided the only thing I could do to cope with my own, self-inflicted misfortune was to write a chapter about my struggles. If nothing else, at least at the end of the day as I am rocking back and forth in a corner sucking my thumb, I can really reach and find some humor in it all.

Below is a list of questions and statements that my darling, five-year-old child utters in a typical hour accompanied by the enharmonic echo of his brother's very raspy, almost-baritone voice. Enjoy:

- Mommy, what is steam?

 - *Steammmm*

- What does evaporate mean?

- How does the water turn to air?

 - *Air! Flyingggggg!*

- Where does it go?

- How does the water molecules get out of the house?

- I want to be a magic maker.

 - *Mag-IC! Mag-IC! Make a dis-e-peer!*

- Mommy, was does uncomfortable mean?

- Zachary isn't helping.

 - *I helping! NO TIME OUT!*

- What does nervous mean?

- How do you spell excited?

 - *Cited! E-cited!*

- Why does the alphabet need uppercase and lowercase letters?

 - Why do you have to vacuum?

 - *Vacuum AJ! Vacuuuum!*

- How does the vacuum suck up dirt?

- Where does the dirt come from?

- Why is there dirt outside?

 - *Oh no! Dirty! It's dirty!*

- Zachary is copying me.
- Zachary is laughing at me.
  - *AJ funny!*
- Zachary took my toy.
  - *My turn! AJ take it!*
- How do they clean the pool?
  - *Pool? Go to the pool?*
- How is a drink made?
- Mommy, I love you.
  - *Love youuuuu!*
- Do dogs have mommies?
- Why do you and daddy have to work?
  - *Mommy go a work?*
- What do we need to have money for?
- How much money do we have?
- How much money was your car?
  - *Car? I car! Get in the car!*
- Zachary is following me.
- Can I play outside?
  - *Shoes on! Go outside!*
- Why is water invisible?
- What does invisible mean?
- Can I call Madi?
  - *Aj! Madi, Madi, Madiii! Ski-nana!*
- When do I get to go back to school?
  - *Aj schoollll, mommy!*
- Mommy, just love you so much.
  - *Love youuuu!*
- When does Daddy come home?
- Why does it rain?
- How big is a cloud?
- How does the cloud keep the rain in?
- Is rain heavy?

- Can I look at my photo book from when I was in your tummy?
   - *Mommy belly!*
- Mommy can we watch the slideshow?
- Mommy, I'm thirsty.
   - *Somethn drank! Somethan DRANKKK!*
- Where does apple juice come from?
- How do the trees get the apples?
   - *Fuit naks! Fooot naks!*
- Do trees grow other juices?
- Does all the food come from trees?
- Mommy, will you sing with me?
   - *Sunshine! Sing it! Sunshine!*
- Why do we have to eat vegetables?
   - *Crae-ots! Want it!*
- Mommy, look what I can do!
   - *I do it too! I do too!*
- Did you just see that?
   - *See it? Mommy, you see it?*
- Mommy, can I take a bath?
   - *Tee-ke bath! Zachary tee-kee bath!*
- Why do you have two names?
- Do I have two names?
- What is Daddy's other name?
- Does MiMi have another name?
   - *Mimi here! Mimi here! Mimi!*
- How does the TV play?
- What does electricity mean?
- Why do we have to pay for the TV?
- Where does money come from?
- Can I call Madi?
   - *Ski-nana! Madi! Go pool?!*
- Can we go outside?

\- Where does the grass come from?

\- Is grass a tree?

\- Why doesn't our grass have flowers?

\- Why is a Pterodactyl in the dinosaur book if it's not a dinosaur?

\- *Dino-Saur!*

\- Why do they put the letter if it's silent?

\- The letter isn't silent. It's a 'P'. It makes a "puh" sound.

\- What other words have "puh" sounds?

\- Do birds live in trees?

.... Are you still reading? Admittedly, I wouldn't be if I were you. I lack the patience.

CHAPTER 8

BANANAS

I AM NEVER BUYING bananas again. I said that once and meant it, even knowing that it was a lie. I really love bananas, but as far as my son knew, we were never buying bananas again. I'm sure you're all wondering why I'd tell such a lie to my son about a harmless fruit, so let me explain how bananas were the source of the most intense feeling of humiliation and stress I've felt in a while.

In the middle of the produce section of a grocery store, I experienced one of those moments where you refuse to allow yourself to look around you, because you know that judgmental eyes are going to make your skin crawl. I usually don't care about what other people think of me. Usually, I go about my business, oblivious to the opinions of others, but on this occasion, I was unable to do that. It was like the earth came to a screeching halt, stopped turning, then centered every ounce of attention on me.

I hated it.

I loathed it.

And, if I have anything to do with it, I swear it will never happen again.

This happened on a day that I went grocery shopping with both of my children, which if you're a mom, you know is like declaring war with your children and attempting to win said war the entire time you're rolling them through the store. Usually, I try to go shopping when my husband is home, so that I can leave the minions with him and shop in peace, but on this particular day, for whatever reason, they were with me.

I have epic tune-out during chaotic spans of time, such as grocery store wars with small boys and usually can navigate my way through aisles filled with kiddy treasure easily. This day was different. This day was the epitome of toddler hell as my son had the mother of all grocery store meltdowns.

We were almost finished shopping, which honestly, I think is the part of this story that frustrates me the most. I was so close to exiting the battle field, that stupid race car shopping cart was so full that I was having trouble pushing it because it was freaking heavy and unreasonably long, then BAM, it happened. I lost the war.

I entered the produce section, stopping first at the bananas. I grabbed a smaller bunch of bananas, and placed them on top of the enormous pile of groceries I had created. Zachary immediately started to yell, "Get them! Get them!"

Momentarily confused, because my kids *know better* than to shout in public places, I gave him the mommy glare. You know, the one that tells him that what he is doing at that current moment is absolutely wrong and to stop immediately—*or else*. I am the master of the mommy glare, especially when we're in public. My kids know, when mommy gives you *that* look, you better stop. Period.

Well, my mommy glare did nothing to stop him from

yelling. I was horrified as he continued shrieking, "Get them! Bannnaaaannnaaassssss!"

I narrowed my eyes at him, then told him using my very low, very quiet, scary mom voice not to yell in the store. I demanded he use his inside voice, then started to push the cart away, assuming that I had succeeded in taming the beast and could deal with him later, you know, after we paid and left the damn store.

At the age of two, my son had a surprisingly deep voice, so his shriek of "NOOOO!" could likely be heard from the Mexican restaurant next door and quite possibly rattled the automatic glass doors.

I was barely a step away from the bananas when he stood up and tried to climb out of his seat. "Bananassss!" he screamed. "Bananas! Mommmmmy! Bananas! Get all them! Get them all!"

Of course now, everyone was looking at me, judging me as I stood there in my paint splattered yoga pants and hoodie, taking in my messy bun and tired eyes, silently chastising me for allowing my son to scream like that in the store.

Quickly, I grabbed Zachary by his shoulders to steady him, then swiped my hands under his feet, forcing his chubby butt right back into the seat. Still gripping his shoulders, I reprimanded him right there in front of my audience.

AJ of course chose that time to chime in, "Mommy, I think he wants bananas."

I glared at AJ, as I continued to force Zachary to sit down. I'm not sure how it was possible, but his screaming only got louder. "Nooooo! Bananas, Mommy! Get them! All them! I need ALLLLLL! Bananasssss!"

I was so frustrated, and so angry that I could have spit and lit all the damn bananas on fire. Why do toddlers choose public places to melt down like this? Why not have this take place at home? Sure, all parents know that temper tantrums are just a normal part of toddler-hood, but dammit, when the tantrums come, you're still judged fiercely and it's still humiliating as hell.

I wasn't able to move the race car cart away from the stupid bananas for what felt like an eternity, because every time I tried to push it forward, Zachary was trying to stand up and climb out of it.

And before you assume that I didn't buckle him in, let me just tell you that I did. I always buckle him in, not that it really matters. He knows how to unbuckle himself and can do it in a flash. Those stupid buckles serve no purpose when you have a kid like Zachary.

Finally, after enduring his screeching for long enough, I grabbed him in my arms like a football, then demanded that AJ get out of the cart. Poor sweet AJ seemed just as mortified as I was.

I walked away from my full cart of groceries, with Zachary beneath my arm, kicking his legs so hard that he was hitting me in my lower back. It was that moment, while I was walking past the wine aisle that I understood why parents become drunks. I saw with real clarity why they choose to drink their way into oblivion. It was then that I understood how it's possible for mothers to snap and want to drive their kids into the ocean or shake them until their little heads rattle. It's because children like my Zachary push you so close to the edge of sanity, leaving you teetering and grasping for even a shred of control.

I wanted to take him into both of my arms, and yell in his face to STOP FREAKING SCREAMING AND SHUT UPPPPPPPP!

But, I didn't. I kept my mouth firmly shut, until I got to

the customer service desk and had to tell the frightened lady that I abandoned a full cart of groceries.

Sorry lady.

I carried my screaming child out to the car and utilized every bit of my self control the entire way. I wanted to throttle him. I wanted to slam him down into his seat and search frantically for some duct tape so silence him.

Once we walked what felt like ten miles to my car, I quickly ushered AJ inside, then put Zachary in his seat and had to use all of my muscles to hold him down so that I could buckle him. He was bucking and thrashing and still squealing about bananas and how he wanted them all.

Once he was buckled, I shut the door and leaned against my car for a minute so that I could take a deep breath. I felt a little bad for making AJ sit in the car listening to him scream.

Once I felt slightly more calm, and less like a lunatic that wanted to duct tape her kid's mouth shut, I jerked open the car door, leaned in super close to his face, grabbed his chin and spoke to him in what I hoped was the most horrifying tone he'd ever heard.

My octave was so low that it could have been a baritone whisper as I looked him directly in his eyes, squeezing his chin between my fingers just enough to get his full attention.

"Stop. Screaming. Now."

That's all I said... and poof, he stopped.

It's hard to admit, but I really think him stopping so instantly really ticked me off. I mean, really? Why couldn't he stop that way when I was in the store? Why the theatrics?

It was like he was mocking me. Probably giving me a stinky little toddler smirk as soon as I shut the car door.

I considered going back into the store, but I couldn't face the people in there. My pride wouldn't allow me. I made my decision, I pulled his crazy ass back out to the car to make a point, so, I needed to stick to my guns.

He wanted *all* the bananas and he thought his demented little toddler tantrum would help him get his way. Well guess what kiddo? Now you get *no* bananas.

o Zachary

1 Mommy

... *I think.*

CHAPTER 9

THEY SAID I
COULDN'T MESS IT UP

THERE ARE many things in this life that I've been able to *fudge* or *wing* or *stumble through.* I discovered I could paint on complete accident. I discovered that I could write by keeping a diary. I usually can figure out things if I set my mind to it. Except, of course, anything that is even remotely domesticated. Like, cooking, baking, sewing or cutting my child's hair.

I knew before this tragedy took place that I shouldn't have attempted it. I even tried to talk myself out of it. But, after being convinced by my darling husband that we would not only save money, but time, I decided to at least give it a try.

You're probably wondering what I'm talking about. You're probably imagining something super complicated or challenging that I failed because it had too many confusing steps to follow.

Let me go ahead and tell you that you're wrong. You're so completely wrong. There weren't any steps or confusing directions. Apparently, from what I'm told, what I attempted is fairly simple for anyone who isn't me.

The tragedy that occurred, that I wasn't supposed to be able to mess up, was a simple haircut for my AJ. A haircut, using clippers with the little plastic guard on the end that is *supposed* to prevent people like me from hacking hair like machete-cut bushes.

I swear I did it right, although my husband insists that I couldn't have possibly. I put the stupid clip thing on and ran the clippers across his hair timidly. I was so gentle and cautious. I was really doing well at first too. Really, I was.

Then, well... I'm not sure how exactly it happened. There I was, just clipping away, feeling pretty darn proud of myself too.

Man, this is so easy! I thought. *And to think, I've been paying somebody to do this the entire time. I could have saved hundreds of dollars. I think I'll do this from now— Oh my god, no!*

My train of completely incorrect thoughts halted immediately as I focused my eyes on my son's scalp.

Oh my god! I scalped my son!

His paper white scalp was showing right there in the front of his head. Of course I couldn't have messed up on the back of his head where it wasn't as noticeable. No, no, no. When I mess up, it's as though my failure is screaming loud and proud, "Look at me! Krista freaking sucks at something!"

Oh, and did I mention that school was starting in a week? His first day of kindergarten was one week away and my son was missing a quarter sized amount of hair, right above his forehead.

"Mommy, what's wrong?" AJ asked me, probably reacting to the horror-stricken look on my face.

I swallowed down my panic, smiled, and lied. Of course I told him everything was fine, you know, since Mommy is super awesome and since I didn't want him to rat me out. I couldn't be honest and tell him, "Well son, your mommy chopped a huge chunk of your hair off." AJ is so reactionary, he knows how to use FaceTime, he would have called his MiMi in three seconds flat to tell on me.

God, I'm never going to live this down. I'm the worst stay-at-home-mom ever.

Eventually, I had to work up the courage to tell my husband, who howled and laughed at me for so long that he almost cried.

Almost cried.

I however, *did* cry when he shaved off my baby's hair. Poor sweet AJ has a big ole' round head, and should never, ever, walk around with a buzzed head. Thanks to his super fantastic mom, his head was shaved and he looked like a cartoon for weeks.

I felt like I should hashtag the whole thing.

#MomFail

CHAPTER 10

I JUST WANTED
TO BAKE A PIE

AS YOU AGE, you begin to really know yourself. The real you, not the you who changes your hair style and favorite color every time your friends do, but the you that is humiliatingly flawed in a quirky, kinda-perfect way that makes you just lovable enough to keep some of your friends. And by friends I mean your family and that one friend that is equally as flawed as you are and is basically considered family anyway.

As I approach my thirties, I've realized that I think I know myself and I finally came to this startling realization over the tattered remnants of a pie carcass. This realization was an epiphany of sorts that hit me like a brick to the face, which is why I decided it was chapter worthy.

Standing there, in my flour covered kitchen, I decided that throwing what was left of this attempt of an apple pie across the room wasn't going to make me feel better, so writing a chapter about what just took place was the next best thing.

As far as my husband is concerned, becoming a stay at home mom meant that I needed to rise to the occasion and become the perfect blend of Betty Crocker and Aunt Jemima, or so I thought. This was before my epiphany, before my moment of crystal clarity and instead during the days of ill-educated, optimistic thoughts about perfectly shaped apple pies and layered cakes. All of these impossible ideas were being concocted by a me, a crazy woman wearing rose colored glasses, one who simply didn't know who she really was, not until she inhaled too much flour and saw the light.

While it was challenging, throughout this journey into what I like to call, "Stay-at-home-mom-hood," I conquered most of the regular cooking. Yeah, sure, let's be honest... Aunt Jemima may laugh in my face at my failed attempts to make her delicious food, but at least most... errr... *some* of my dinners are edible at this point. I have learned the delicate art of making slimy, vein-filled meat look less like animal carcass and more like actual food a person might want to eat.

What I cannot manage to do, despite my best efforts, is rise to the occasion and bake anything that can even be considered edible, much less a pastry. I absolutely cannot consider myself the new Betty Crocker, I do not channel her when I enter my kitchen... hell, I don't even channel her second cousin twice removed. Oh no, not me. I am the Betty Crocker hater with a grudge against all things considered a pastry with kitchen-rage issues. Why do you ask? Let's talk about that, shall we?

First of all, why exactly does baking have to be so complicated? I think I've adequately covered this in previous chapters, but it's still bugging me. I mean seriously, let's just back up a minute and think about what a person has to go through before even entering their kitchen to begin their failed attempt at baking. Let's start at the grocery store.

Yes, that's a good place to start... let's start at *my* grocery store visit after I decided to make my husband an apple pie.

So, I walked into the store with both of my boys sitting in one of those ridiculous race car grocery carts. You know, the ones that won't push straight and usually knock over the fancy displays that block the aisle ways when you try to turn. I am already stressed as I put my entire body weight against this wretched cart and try to maneuver it over to the produce section in search of fresh apples. Apparently, one cannot make an apple pie with the canned apples on the baking aisle, no, no, no, you have to use the fresh ones in the produce section. I learned that at least during my last failed attempt to make a pie.

So, I finally made it to the apples after telling the boys no fifty billion times in response to their fifty billion questions. In route, of course, I had to pass cookies, cakes, balloons and freaking summer beach toys, all of which were on the boys must-have list. It was basically a declaration of war ignoring their attempts to beg and bargain as I made a bee-line for these apples. As I stood in front of them, I felt immediately overwhelmed and my palms began to sweat a bit. My mind started to race...

Oh my god, there are loose apples and bagged apples. There are gala apples, granny smith apples, these yellow ones that are missing the stupid label. Damn, I bet those are the ones I need, the ones that I can't know for sure if they're right, that would be my luck. Okay, focus... red delicious apples, fuji apples, honey crisp... ummm, golden delicious? Why are there so many? An apple is a damn apple right? Don't they all taste basically the same? Which one is right?

So, I pulled out my phone to look up this random recipe that I found on the internet. I groaned at my warning message indicating that I was roaming and silently prayed that the recipe pulled up.

I finally found the recipe, just when AJ started moaning that he needed to use the restroom, which was conveniently located on the other side of the store. Groaning internally, I pushed my race car out of the produce section and back into the land of temptation, prompting Zachary to start shouting, "Balloon! Mommy! BALLOOOOONNNN!"

Ignoring his repeated outburst, I pushed on, pretending that I was not aware of the polished woman wearing too-heavy earrings staring at me with judgmental eyes.

What is her problem anyway? So what, I left the house in flip flops and my usual paint-stained yoga pants. So what if I'm walking through a public place with a ninja-turtle Band-Aid on my t-shirt. My kid thought it was a sticker and would have melted down if I took it off... I must pick my battles and not everyone is privileged enough to leave the house with a fancy-pants hair-do and too much make up.

I finally made it to the bathroom after passing a display of donuts and more summer toys for the boys to squeal about. I spent the time in the bathroom, fussing at Zachary not to touch the floor and asking AJ not to sing so loud because we're in public. I seriously considered abandoning my pie mission all together, but reconsidered after reminding myself that I took the time to come all the way to the store, with the kids I might add, so I might as well follow through.

I battled my way back to the apples and discovered that my recipe called for tart apples and of course, there wasn't a single label indicating that any of the apple types available to me at that particular moment were tart.

Now what do I do? Why does it have to be so hard, why can't it just say red apple or green apple?

I decided to google the types of apples that are considered tart apples. After watching my internet load for what felt like a year, I gave up and let AJ pick a bag of apples. I mean really, could they really taste that different? And, if they do I just don't care enough to fret over it any longer so I move on to the next ingredient: Shortening.

I pushed my race car away from produce in the direction of the shelf items, then came to a stop as I realized that I have no idea where shortening would be. What is shortening anyway? It's probably on the baking aisle, so I head that way and immediately look at the sign. Of course shortening isn't listed but I walk down the aisle anyway, ignoring my knee jerk reaction to bolt in the other direction. I hate the baking aisle, it makes me anxious and nervous. I feel like all the pro-moms that bake from scratch one-handed with their eyes closed are laughing at me while I fret over canned icing flavors. I feel pressured to make my decisions quickly so that I look like I know what I'm doing, even if what I am doing is completely elementary in comparison.

Anyway, so I headed deep into the backing aisle looking for shortening and I started to panic a little as I reached the end of the aisle without seeing anything with that word on it. I couldn't possibly turn around and back track, because that would have made me look like an idiot, so I just went to the next aisle and pretended to look for something else while googling shortening to figure out what the hell it actually is.

Of course the next aisle is the cookie and cracker aisle, prompting the volume of my children's squeals to increase to an embarrassing level. I felt frustrated watching my internet fail to load while using my quiet, scary-mom voice to reprimand my children so that they'd stop screaming for cookies as we walked away from them. Reaching the end of the aisle, I reloaded my browser again feeling closer to giving up.

How important can shortening be anyway? I'm sure I can make the pie without it.

Deciding that I was far too confused to continue on my search for shortening, I quickly gathered the remaining ingredients. You know, the ones that made sense to me like flour, salt and cinnamon. After paying, I took my loud mouth kids back to the house while still maintaining my cool as I listened to them whine about not getting anything from the store.

After getting the kids settled on the couch with a movie, I made my way to the kitchen feeling surprisingly eager to make this stupid pie that my husband loves so much. I blanched at the first line of directions, "In a medium bowl, mix two cups of flour and one teaspoon of salt. Cut in shortening using a pastry blender."

Realizing that I should have toughed it out and figured out what shortening was made me feel irritated at myself, but that wasn't the problem at hand that made my face ashen. No, the problem was two simple words: Cut. In. *What does "cut in" mean anyway? How do you cut something into another ingredient?*

Now that I was no longer roaming, I pulled out my phone to google shortening which results in a significant increase in my irritation. Apparently shortening is just vegetable oil in a solid form, something I actually did pass on the baking aisle. Why did I pass it you ask? Oh, only because it doesn't say "shortening" on the label. I mean, why would it say what it actually is? That would make it simple. No, they have to leave that word out so that baking morons like myself walk around feeling clueless and angry at a grocery store.

After puttering around in my pantry and refrigerator, I found some shortening. I am sure my husband or one of my friends must have purchased it because I certainly didn't. I reread the first part of the directions and blanche again.

I don't have a pastry blender and I don't know what "cut in" means, so I'm not sure what to do.

I'll just mix it in normally, I'm sure "cut in" is just a fancy baking way to say mix. But wait, it didn't say how much... How much shortening do I put, why didn't it say?

I study the recipe again, scrolling back up to the top to find the amount. It says, "Two-thirds of a cup plus two tablespoons shortening."

A long moment of confused silence immediately took place in my kitchen.

So, do I put in two-thirds of a cup or two tablespoons? Why is it written like that? Why not include the two table-spoons in the initial measurement?

My confusion was interrupted by my child yelling that he pooped and needed me to wipe his butt. I'm certain that I've never been more excited about wiping a child's butt, so I gleefully wiped off my hands and abandoned my confused mission.

After tending to my child's bathroom break, I found my way back to the kitchen deciding to just put all the short-ening in at once. I mixed it up and went on to the next part of the instructions. Apparently I was supposed to be seeing pea sized particles but, all I saw was a big, sticky, very messy, ball of goop.

Is this supposed to end up being the crust? What am I making?

My frustration increased as flour puffed into the air with each attempt to mix it into the shortening. Half of it was super slimy and gooey and the other half was still loose flour.

The next part of the recipe said to sprinkle cold water onto it until the entire pastry was moist and it cleans the side of the bowl. That seems easy enough, right? Well no... it's not. I sprinkled water and tried to mix, then sprinkled again.

How much water do I sprinkle? It doesn't say... it just says, "Until moist and cleans the bowl."

I continued sprinkling, never seeming to reach the desired result. Instead I managed to make a paste that was thicker in some areas and loose in others.

I sighed loudly, prompting my five-year-old to ask what I'm doing. I stopped sprinkling water and squeezed the bridge of my nose, immediately realizing that my hands were coated in this gooey paste that I'd created.

Great, so now I have pie goo on my face.

"Mommy, what are you doing? What is on your face? What is this?"

Before I could stop him, AJ had put his hands into my bowl of goo. Trying to find my mommy-zen, I pulled him away from my pie goo and towards the kitchen sink. While we washed our hands together, I told him that Mommy is trying to bake a pie. His response annoyed me, "Mommy! That doesn't look like a pie!" I explained that it isn't cooked yet, so it still looks like ingredients knowing that it will probably forever just look like ingredients. I knew that I'd never pull it off.

Gazing down at my goo ball, I decided to add more flour to make it less of a paste and more of a... crust?

Obviously, my idea didn't work and I seriously considered slinging the entire mixing bowl and its contents across my kitchen but then stopped suddenly.

This is the moment of clarity I was talking about. The moment when I just accepted that I cannot do this. I am not Susie Homemaker. Who am I kidding? I hate baking. I cannot pull myself out of my confused, frustrated state of mind to find any enjoyment in this. And why would I want to do this anyway? Who wants to battle the grocery store war with two needy boys in a race car cart that refuses to drive straight, just to come home and try to make sense of ridiculous, fragmented directions that only result in the grossest looking paste you've ever seen? Not this girl.

This just isn't me, it isn't. I can do a lot of things and have mastered many talents, but I simply cannot bake and that's okay with me.

I'm the girl who wears clothes that are covered in paint, who always has thirty different projects going on at once, who belts out soulful music while effortlessly mixing three different shades of blue paint to create cerulean. I'm the girl who isn't ashamed to admit that she gleefully loves Disney movies so much that she paints scenes from the movies on a daily basis. I'm the girl who loves to write novels about worlds that don't actually exist, who falls in love with the characters in her stories so deeply that she grieves them after the story has ended.

I'm the girl who pees her pants watching scary movies and hates to be tickled. I'm the girl who looks at the world through the eyes of a photographer, finding something beautiful in even the grittiest places. I'm the girl who owns make-up but cannot remember where it is, who can't stand the thought of color coating her nails and sometimes forgets to brush her hair in the morning before piling it on top of her head in a messy bun.

I'm the girl who isn't bothered by imperfection or a mess, the girl who feels most at ease amongst chaos. I'm the girl who would rather have cheap flip-flops on and mud between her toes than stilettos on her feet. I'm the girl who plans things months in advance and never gets lost because she has maps residing in her head. I'm the girl who snaps her fingers when she dances, who listens to everything from Spice Girls, to Elton John to Michael Jackson, who buys outfits for her children with a themed photo session in mind. I'm the girl who is loud and silly often and gets excited at menial things.

I've realized that my creativity dominates who I am and I think I'm okay with that. I cannot sew, I can barely cook and I certainly cannot bake. I am a mom that would rather order take out and finger paint with her kids then make cookies.

I'll never be Susie Homemaker or a Betty Crocker reincarnate... I am a messy, quirky artist with Type-A tendencies who craves projects like it's air to breathe. I think relaxing is a waste of time and cannot figure out how to do it. I create memories with acrylic paint, crayons and the laughter of my children then relive them through the the pictures I can't seem to stop taking.

So, the pie goo ended up in the trash and I vow to never attempt another. It's not who I am... I can't bake and I am no longer interested in trying.

I was born to be a motivated, art loving, book writing mom.

That's me and I'm proud of it.

THANK YOU FOR READING!

I hope my story provided you with a little bit of laughter in the midst of what is probably a very hectic life.

Please, leave a review.

OTHER BOOKS BY KRISTA GARRAND

<u>Blood Bonds Series:</u>

Unbound Reverie

The Pull

The Bond

Boundless

The Beseeching

Dear Life

You Heal my Heart

UPCOMING WORKS BY KRISTA

<u>The Heart Trilogy:</u>
You Heal My Heart,
You Still My Heart,
You Calm My Heart

<u>The Destiny Duet:</u>
Kismet, Fortuity

The Hush

It's Alright

Be Still

Mercy

MORE ON THIS AUTHOR

KRISTA GARRAND LIVES in a rural town on the outskirts of Charleston, SC with her husband, five boys and one little girl. When she isn't writing, she's immersed in her children, planning camping trips or traveling. Beyond reading and writing, she enjoys painting and running her photography business.

WANT TO FOLLOW HER?

Find her here:

www.authorkristagarrand.com

Loudhouse Press

Cover Designer: GermanCreative

Editor: Christi Humbertson

Content Editors: Angela Kolwyck, Melanie Salter

eBook ISBN: 979-8-950588-06-8

ISBN: 979-8-950588-07-5

Printed in USA | Second Edition May 2026 |

10 9 8 7 6 5 4 3 2